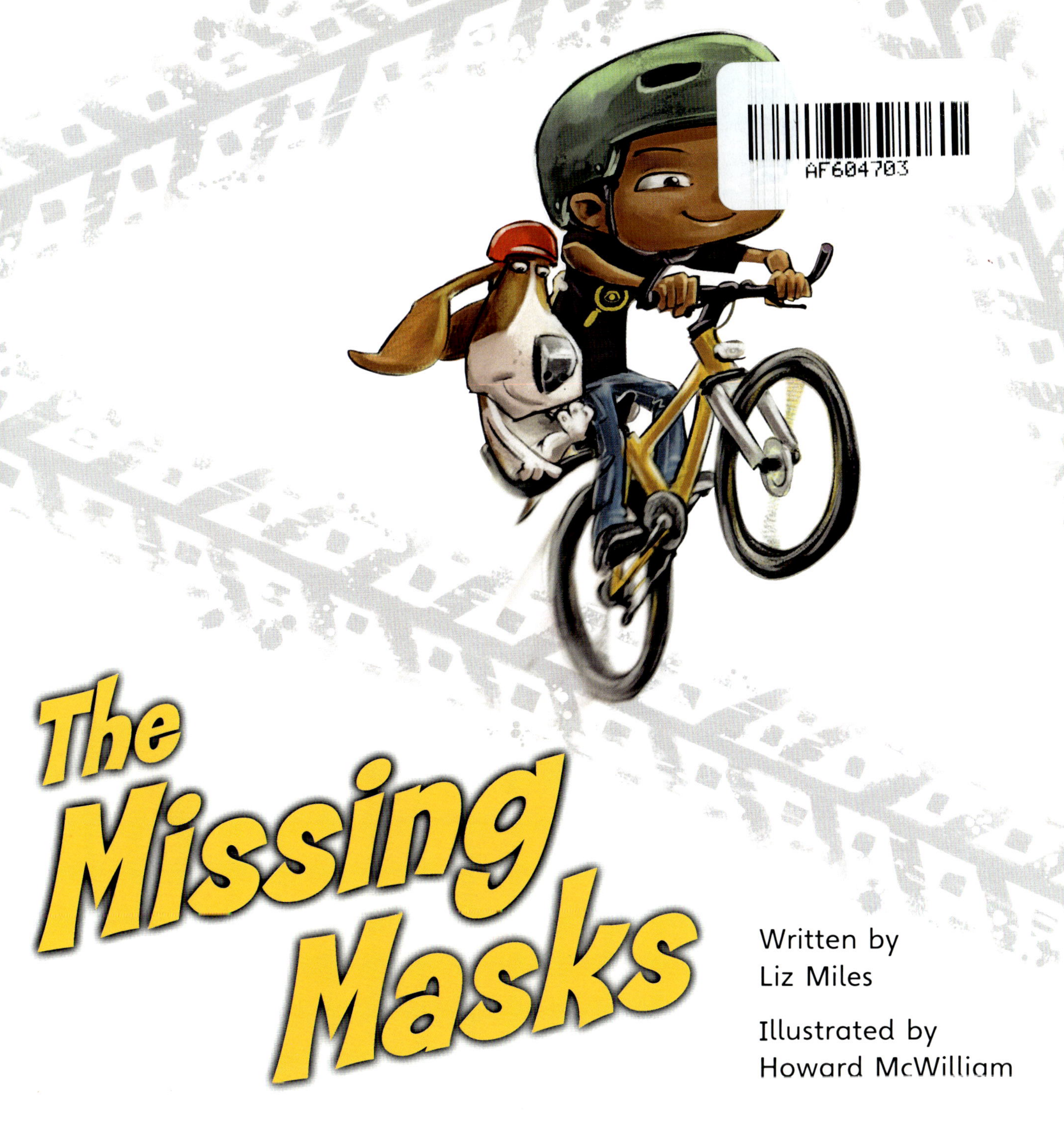

The Missing Masks

Written by
Liz Miles

Illustrated by
Howard McWilliam

In this story:

Jay

Sniffer

Mr Slime

The teacher

The school hall got very wet.

Mr Slime

The teacher

The school hall got very wet.

"It will cost a lot to fix the hall,"
said the teacher.
"We will have to shut the school."

"Let's put on a play," said Jay. "We can put on masks! People will pay a lot to see the play. Then we can fix the hall!"

"I will take the masks and stop the play," said Mr Slime.

"Then the school will shut
and I can put a hotel here!
People will pay a lot
to stay in it."

It was the day of the play.
The children went to get their masks.

"Oh no! Where are the masks?" said Jay.
Just then, there was a sneeze.

"Oh no! Mr Slime has got the masks!" said Jay.

"Quick, Sniffer! Let's get him!"

Jay got on his bike.
Sniffer got on, too.
They followed Mr Slime into the park.

"Get him, Sniffer!" said Jay.

Mr Slime let go of the masks.
He fell into the pond.

"This is a good place for the play!" said Jay.

"People will pay a lot to see it here. Thank you, Mr Slime!"